GETTING TO KNOW THE WORLD'S GREATEST ARTISTS

PICASSO

WRITTEN AND ILLUSTRATED BY MIKE VENEZIA

CHILDRENS PRESS ®

CHICAGO

To Pat and Gene with love

*The author wishes to express a special thanks
to Sarah Mollman*

Cover: Boy in Sailor Suit with Butterfly Net. 1938. Phototheque, SPADEM/Art Resource

Library of Congress Cataloging-in-Publication Data

Venezia, Mike.
    Picasso / written and illustrated by Mike Venezia.
        p.   cm. — (Getting to know the world's greatest
artists)
    Summary: Briefly examines the life and work of the
renowned twentieth-century artist, describing and giving
examples from his various periods or styles.
    ISBN 0-516-02271-7
    1. Picasso, Pablo, 1881-1973—Juvenile
literature. 2.   Painters—France—Biography—Juvenile
literature. 3. Painting. French—Juvenile
literature. 4.   Painting. Modern—19th century—
France—Juvenile literature. 5.   Painting, Modern—20th
century—France—Juvenile literature. [1.   Picasso,
Pablo, 1881-1973. 2.   Artists. 3.   Painting,
French. 4.   Painting, Modern—France. 5.   Art
appreciation.] I.   Picasso, Pablo, 1881-
1973. II. Title. II. Series.
ND553.P5V35   1988   87-33023
759.4—dc19   CIP
[92]   AC

Childrens Press®, Chicago
Copyright ©1988 by Regensteiner Publishing Enterprises, Inc.
All rights reserved. Published simultaneously in Canada.
Printed in the United States of America.
    9 10 R 97 96

Pablo Picasso. New York, AP/Wide World Photos, Inc.

Pablo Picasso was one of the greatest artists of the twentieth century. He was born in Malaga, Spain, in 1881, and died in France in 1973.

Picasso's father was an art teacher
at the local school. He encouraged his

son to paint and draw. He wanted
Picasso to become a great artist
some day.

The Altar Boy. 1896. Canvas.
Spain, Courtesy Abadia de Montserrat, Barcelona

Picasso's painting style changed over the period of his life more than any other great artist. He was always trying new and different things.

The painting above was done when he was only fifteen years old.

Boy in Sailor Suit with Butterfly Net. 1938.
Phototheque, SPADEM/Art Resource

This painting was done when
Picasso was fifty-seven.

There's quite a difference between
the two paintings, isn't there?

Girl Before a Mirror. 1932. Canvas, 162.3 x 130.2 cm. New York, The Museum of Modern Art

Sometimes Picasso would paint things that looked very flat.

Bather with a Beach Ball. 1932. Canvas, 146.2 x 114.6 cm.
New York, The Museum of Modern Art

Sometimes he would paint things that looked so round that you might be able to pick them up off the painting.

When Picasso was nineteen, he left Spain and went to Paris, France. Some of the first paintings he did there look a little bit like the work of other famous French artists.

This painting reminds many people of the work done by Toulouse-Lautrec. Some of Picasso's other early paintings remind people of Van Gogh, Gauguin, and Monet.

Le Moulin de la Galette. 1900. Canvas, 90 x 2 x 117 cm. New York, Solomon R. Guggenheim Museum

11

THE BLUE PERIOD

Then something happened! Picasso's paintings changed. His work became different from anyone else's.

His best friend died, and Picasso felt alone and sad. At the same time, none of his paintings were selling, and he was almost starving to death.

Because of his mood, Picasso began to paint with lots of blue (blue can be a very sad color). He made all the people in his paintings look lonely and sad.

The Old Guitarist. 1903. Panel, 122.9 x 82.6 cm. The Art Institute of Chicago

Some people thought Picasso's blue paintings were great. Others (including Picasso's father) thought they were just too strange. This meant his paintings were controversial.

THE ROSE PERIOD

Picasso's Blue Period ended when
he met a girl named Fernande.
Fernande and Picasso fell in love, and
soon a happier color started showing
up in Picasso's paintings. This was
the beginning of the Rose Period.

Family of Saltimbanques. 1905. Canvas, 212.8 x 229.6 cm. Washington , D.C., National Gallery of Art

Not only were Picasso's colors happier during the Rose Period, but he started painting happier things. Picasso painted a lot of circus people during this time. He often painted them with their animals.

The Rose Period didn't last very long, though, because Picasso found a new way to paint that was really exciting and different.

Portrait of D. H. Kahnweiler. 1910. Canvas, 100.6 x 72.8 cm. The Art Institute of Chicago

CUBISM

Cubism was the next style of painting that Picasso developed and made famous.

This is a cubist painting of one of Picasso's friends. The man in the painting looks like he's been broken up into little cubes. That's where the name cubism came from.

Look closely. Can you see the man's face, what he was wearing, his hands, a bottle, a glass, and maybe his pet cat? Can you find anything else?

Cubism is one of the most
important periods in the history of
modern art.

For hundreds of years, artists tried
very hard to paint things so they
would look real. Then Picasso came
along and started to paint people and

things that didn't look the way
people and things were supposed to
look.

Picasso was always shocking
people, but when he started painting
people who had eyes and noses in the
wrong places—well, even some of his
closest friends thought he had gone
too far.

Picasso kept working with cubism and changed it over the years. It became much more colorful and flatter looking. It also became easier to see what Picasso was painting.

In the painting *Three Musicians*, you can see the three musicians, and tell what instruments they're playing.

In another style that popped up for a while, Picasso painted people who looked more real again. Picasso had

Three Musicians. 1921. Canvas, 200.7 x 222.9 cm. New York, The Museum of Modern Art

Three Women at the Spring. 1921. Canvas, 203.9 x 174 cm.
New York, The Museum of Modern Art

just visited Rome, a city filled with
statues and monuments. When he
returned from his trip, he did a series
of paintings in which people look like
they've been chiseled out of stone,
like statues.

GUERNICA

In 1937 something happened that made Picasso paint his most powerful and serious painting.

During a civil war that was going on in Spain, the small town of Guernica was destroyed by bombs. Thousands of innocent people were killed or injured.

Picasso became very angry and used everything he knew to make a painting that would show the world how foolish war was. He named the painting after the town that was destroyed.

Guernica. 1937.Canvas, 351 x 782 cm. Madrid, Museo del Prado

Picasso used darker colors, cubism,
and lots of expression to get his
angry feelings across in this painting.

He also used size. This painting is
huge. It's 12 feet high and 25 feet
wide!

Portrait of Jaime Sabartés as a Spanish Grandee. 1939. Canvas, 46 x 38 cm. Spain, Picasso Museum

Many of Picasso's paintings look funny because of the way he moves eyes, noses, and chins around. The amazing thing about these paintings is how much they look like the real person.

Look at the painting of Picasso's best friend, Jaime Sabartés, on the opposite page. Does it look like the same man shown in the painting below?

Jaime Sabartés, painted by Steve Dobson, from a photograph by Gilberte Brassai

The thing that made Picasso such a great artist was his originality. He had the imagination to try new and different things through his entire life.

The Old Fisherman. 1895.
Canvas, 82 x 62 cm. Courtesy Abadia
de Montserrat, Barcelona

The Ape and Her Young. 1952.
Sculpture. Paris, Musee Picasso.
Giraudon/Art Resource

Minotauromachia. 1935.
Etching, 49.2 x 69 cm.
The Art Institute of Chicago

Weeping Woman. 1937.
Canvas, 60 x 49 cm. London,
The Bridgeman Art Library/Art Resource

Four Children Viewing a Monster.
1933. Etching, 33.5 x 44.8 cm.
The Art Institute of Chicago

Picasso lived to be ninety-two
years old. He was a great painter, but
he was great at other things, too.

He made sculptures, prints,
drawings, beautifully colored dishes
and bowls. He even made costumes
and scenery for plays.

It's a lot of fun to see real Picasso paintings. You'll be surprised at how big some of them are. Look for his paintings in your art museum.

The pictures in this book came from the museums listed below. If none of these museums is close to you, maybe you can visit one when you are on vacation.

Abadia de Montserrat, Barcelona, Spain

The Museum of Modern Art, New York, New York

Solomon R. Guggenheim Museum, New York, New York

The Art Institute, Chicago, Illinois

National Gallery of Art, Washington, D. C.

Museo del Prado, Madrid, Spain

Picasso Museum, Barcelona, Spain

Musee Picasso, Paris, France